MW00714701

A Child's Story of Canada

Copyright 2003 © Karin Moorhouse and Penumbra Press
Printed and bound in Canada.
This volume is a second edition published by Penumbra Press, and is
based on the first edition published by Penumbra Press in 1983 and
reprinted in 1985.

No part of this publication may be reproduced, stored in a retrieval
system or transmitted, in any form or by any means, without the
prior written consent of the publisher or a licence from the The
Canadian Copyright Licensing Agency (Access Copyright).
For an Access Copyright licence, call toll free to 1-800-893-5777 or visit
www.accesscopyright.ca.

NATIONAL LIBRARY OF CANADA CATALOGUING IN PUBLICATION
Moorhouse, Karin
   A child's story of Canada / text and illustrations by Karin
Moorhouse. — 2nd ed.
ISBN 1-894131-47-9
   1. Canada--History--Juvenile literature. I. Title.

FC58..M66 2003   j971   C2003-903249-3   F1008.2 M66 2003

PENUMBRA PRESS gratefully acknowledges the Canada Council for the
Arts and the Ontario Arts Council for supporting their publishing
programme. The publisher further acknowledges the financial sup-
port of the Government of Canada through the Book Publishing
Industry Development Program (BPIDP) for our publishing activities.
We also acknowledge the Government of Ontario through the
Ontario Media Development Corporation's Ontario Book Initiative.

Visit our website to browse other children's books,
www.penumbrapress.com

A Child's Story of Canada

Text and illustrations by Karin Moorhouse

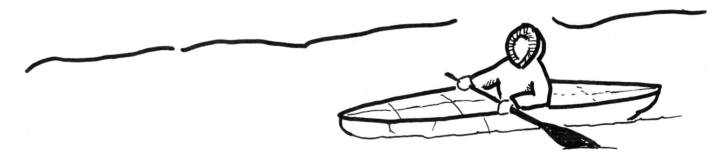

Penumbra Press

Dedicated to my grandchildren, the children I have taught and to all those who may come to read this book.

For the administrators of the Stewart Hall Cultural Centre of the City of Pointe Claire, Québec, who have encouraged me over the years to tell the story of Canada to so many young children.

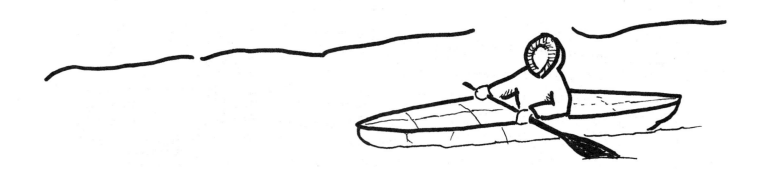

Eskimos: The first Canadians were the Eskimos and the Indians. The Eskimos lived along the Arctic shores. In the winter they made their houses of snow because they had no wood. They hunted seals and used the skins to make their clothes. They ate the seal meat and melted seal fat to make oil for the stone lamps that were used for cooking and heating. Their skin-covered boats were called kayaks and they had dogs to pull their sleds. The arctic winters were bitterly cold, long and dark, but the Eskimos were warm inside their snug igloos. At night they slept on snow benches covered with furs. The oil lamps were kept burning all night long. The Eskimos were friendly, happy people and whatever they had they shared with one another.

West Coast Indians: The Indians who lived along the west coast of Canada between the mountains and the sea had huge trees which they could use to make their homes and boats and totem poles. Because they had no metal tools, they cut down the trees by burning around their base and chopping out the burned wood with stone axes until the trees fell. Then they could split the trees into planks to build homes or hollow out the logs by more burning to make long, heavy canoes.

The Indians liked to decorate the things they used. Their totem poles and canoes were decorated with carvings and paintings.

Life was much easier for the West Coast Indians than for the Eskimos. The trees gave them wood for homes and canoes, and firewood for cooking and heat. There was plenty to eat. They had berries, deer, and small woodland animals, as well as salmon from the seas.

Buffalo Hunters: The Indians who lived on the Plains hunted the buffalo. Because they had to follow the herds around, they lived in tepees which could easily be moved. They ate buffalo meat and used buffalo skins to cover their tepees. When the Indians had a lot of meat they cut it into strips and dried it in the sun so that it would keep.

The Indians never thought of a wheel, so their dogs helped them to carry their belongings when they had to move. The dogs were harnessed to two poles whose ends dragged on the ground. Bundles were tied onto the poles.

There were no horses on the Plains until after the white man came to North America. It was a hard life following the buffalo on foot.

Woodland Indians: The Woodland Indians in the East lived in villages in longhouses. Several families lived in each longhouse and there was a strong fence around the whole village to protect them from the attacks of other Indians. Outside the fence, the Indian women had gardens where they grew corn and pumpkins and beans. The men hunted deer and other animals in the forest and fished in the lakes and rivers. They used birch bark to make canoes that were so light they could easily be carried through the forests and over the trails from one river to another.

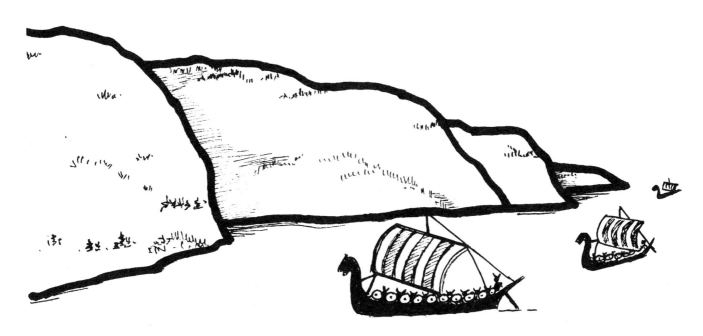

Vikings: The Vikings came to Newfoundland from Greenland in the year 999. They were looking for farmland and for wood to mend their ships. Greenland was so far north that most of it was covered with ice and there were no trees. The first Viking to come to Canada was Leif the Lucky, who stayed only one winter. Then came Karlsefni, who brought one hundred and sixty people and cattle in three ships. The Vikings had so much trouble with the Indians that after three years they went back home to Greenland. The first white child born in Canada was a little Viking boy called 'Snorri.'

John Cabot: After the Vikings left, no more white people came to live in Canada for a long time. But every summer, fishermen from many countries came to fish. They dried the fish or salted it and when their ships were filled, they sailed back to their own countries.

By now, people knew that the earth was round. They knew that China was to the east of them, but they thought that if they kept going west, they would eventually get to China. All the most beautiful things—silks, gold, porcelain—came from China, but these things were very expensive because they had to be carried over mountains and deserts on the backs of horses and camels. Would it be quicker and cheaper to get to China by sailing west?

One day the King of England said to a sea-captain called John Cabot, 'You go and see what you can find over there—perhaps a way through to China or perhaps some land you can claim for England.'

So John Cabot sailed away and the first land he came to he called 'the New Found Isle.' We call it Newfoundland now.

Cabot went ashore on Cape Breton Island, too, and put up a flag to show that the island belonged to England. But he didn't stay long.

Jacques Cartier: In 1534 Jacques Cartier came to the New World from France. He was also looking for a way to China. He went ashore at the Gaspé and claimed the land for the King of France and met some Indians. Cartier and the Indians could not understand each other so he took two of the Indian boys back to France to learn French. On their way home they passed the gulf of a huge river pouring out from the West. Could this be the way to China?

But winter was near and they dared not stay; they sailed back to France and told the King what they had seen.

In the spring Cartier came back to Canada. He sailed straight to the gulf he had seen the year before. He sailed upstream with his three ships to where the river narrowed. There was an Indian village on the top of a cliff; this was the home of the friendly Indians he had met before.

Cartier left his two big ships there with most of the men and told them to build a good warm house in case they had to stay for the winter. Then he sailed upstream until he reached an island with a big hill on it. From the top of the hill he could see that there were fierce rapids that would stop ships from going farther up the river. Disappointed, Cartier went back to Québec, where he had left his men. They decided to spend the winter in the good house they had built there. The winter was very cold and they had no fresh food. Many of the men got sick and died.

When the group finally went back to France in the spring, the King decided not to send any more people to Canada.

Samuel de Champlain: Some years later the French came to Canada again. Their leader was Samuel de Champlain. 'We can't keep running back to France every winter,' he said and built a strong house called the 'Habitation.' It was near the place where Cartier had spent that terrible winter. Champlain called the place 'Québec' after the Indian name 'Kebec.'

Champlain made friends with some Algonquin Indians who helped him to explore all the way to Lake Huron. They went by canoe up the St. Lawrence and Ottawa rivers and then across country to Georgian Bay and Lake Huron.

He was disappointed when the Indians' 'Shining Water' turned out to be, not the sea, but the Great Lakes; but he was pleased with everything else he saw — good land, plenty of trees, animals and fish.

In return, Champlain helped the Algonquins to defeat their old enemy, the Iroquois. From that time on, the Iroquois were the enemies of the French too.

When Champlain told the King that he had found good farm land, the King sent settlers and nuns and missionaries.

After Champlain came there were always French people here and people still call him the 'Father of Canada.'

Fur Trade: The Indians brought furs to the new French settlement and traded them for useful things like axes and knives and blankets and cooking pots. While the French were building and exploring and trading with their Indian friends around the St. Lawrence and Ottawa rivers, the English were building and farming farther south and trading with the Iroquois Indians. The northern furs were better because the animals there grew thicker coats for the colder winters.

Maisonneuve and Montreal: In the year 1642 a soldier called Maisonneuve came from France, bringing a group of 59 people in three ships. They were sure that the Voice of God had told them to go to the Island of Montréal to tell the Indians about Jesus. When they got to Québec, the Governor was shocked. 'Don't go so far away,' he said. 'If the Iroquois attack, we shan't be able to help you.' But Maisonneuve was firm. 'If every tree on the island were an Indian,' he said, 'we would still go.' When the missionaries arrived at Montréal, there was no one living on the island. They were able to build their houses and to put up a strong fence all around the settlement. They hunted and fished and started gardens. In the spring, a party of Iroquois, passing the island on its way to summer fishing grounds, spotted the new French settlement and attacked. From then on there was no peace.

No one could leave the little settlement to hunt or fish until they got a dog called Pilotte, who warned them when the Iroquois were near.

Georgian Bay Missions: Some French missionaries went even farther away and built mission posts among the Huron Indians near Georgian Bay. They took Champlain's old route: up the St. Lawrence and the Ottawa. Then they went across country by smaller rivers, lakes and portages to Georgian Bay on Lake Huron. The Hurons were friendly and liked to hear what the missionaries told them. They showed the French how to make snowshoes and birch bark canoes, which were Indian inventions, and how to grow corn. And they traded their good furs for the metal tools and pots that the French had and which the Indians could not make for themselves.

One day the Iroquois said to themselves, 'Why should those Hurons have all the good furs? We'll attack them and drive them away, and then we'll have the best furs.'

They attacked the Huron villages and burned them and killed the Hurons and the French missionaries. The Hurons who were still alive ran and hid in the forests. The Iroquois were the fiercest of the Indian tribes and after the massacre none of the other tribes dared to come to trade with the French. For more than a year no furs got through to Québec. The French settlers had no furs to send to France to pay for the things they needed—food, clothing, weapons and tools and pots for trading.

Frontenac Defeats Iroquois: The Iroquois wanted to get rid of the French just as they had got rid of the Hurons, and for a long time they kept attacking French farms and villages, burning them and killing the people.

At last the King of France sent a regiment of soldiers to protect the colonists from these attacks. The regiment was called the Carignan-Salière and the people of Québec were happy to see them come ashore from their ships. But trouble with the Iroquois lasted until Frontenac arrived to become Governor at Québec.

He sent the soldiers south to punish the Iroquois by burning their villages and crops. Then he invited the chiefs to a big meeting in order to make peace.

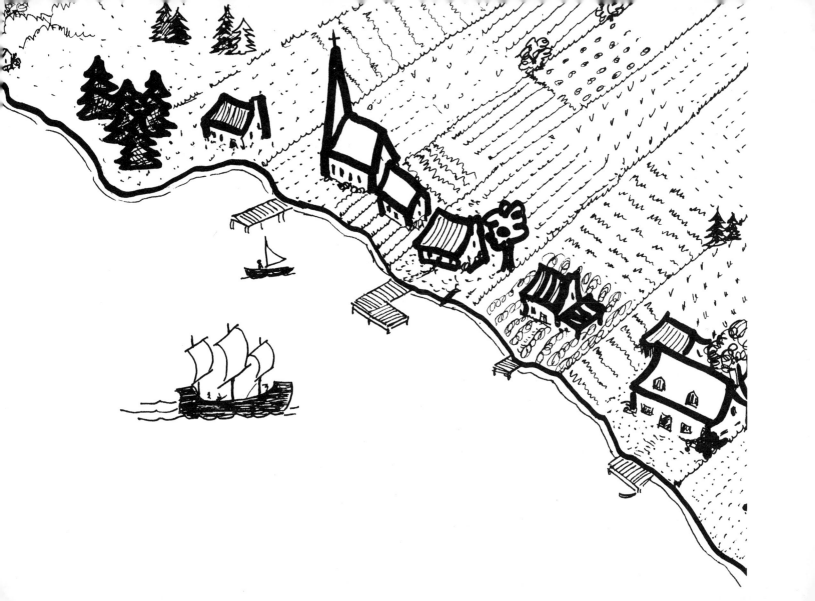

New Settlers: Soon more people began to come from France to settle in Canada — New France they called it.

Farmers came, and traders and missionaries. Then nuns came to look after sick people and to teach the children. Because there were no roads everyone wanted to have his home by the river. It was easier to travel by boat on the water in summer and by sleigh on the ice in winter.

Coureurs de Bois: For a long time after Frontenac had beaten the Iroquois, no Indians brought their furs to the French settlements. Even after the Iroquois went south to trade with the English settlements, the other tribes were still afraid to come. So the French sent out their young men—coureurs de bois, they were called—to trade with the Indians in their own villages. But every year the young men had to go farther as furs were getting scarcer.

The French decided to build fur trading posts along the rivers and lakes, at places where it was easy for the Indians to bring their furs to trade. The French could store their supplies safely at these posts and use them as a base for their hunting and trapping in winter. In the spring, they paddled back to the great fur fairs in Montréal, bringing with them great fleets of canoes loaded with furs.

Discovery of Hudson Bay: Radisson and Groseilliers were two very brave and adventurous young coureurs. Going farther and farther away in search of furs, they came at last to Hudson Bay—the first coureurs to get there by land. As they looked at the sea, they had a good idea. If they had a big sailing ship in Hudson Bay, it could take hundreds of canoe loads of furs directly to Europe by sea. This way would be much quicker and cheaper than taking the furs all the way back to Montréal by canoe and then sending them on by sailing ship.

Radisson and Groseilliers went to France to tell the King about their idea. But he was busy fighting a war and could not spare the ships. The two men then went to England to see King Charles. The King thought it was a splendid idea and loaned them two ships. Radisson's ship was damaged in a storm and had to turn back; Groseilliers' ship—called the *Nonsuch*—got all the way into Hudson Bay, picked up a huge load of furs and sailed back to London. The King was delighted. That was the beginning of the Hudson's Bay Company. The English built fur trading forts on the shores of the Bay and the Indians brought their furs there instead of taking them to the French on the St. Lawrence River.

French and English Troubles: The French were very angry when they heard that the Indians were taking their furs to the English. Nor did they like having the English to the north of them on the Bay and to the south in the English settlements so they sent their best soldier, D'Iberville, overland to attack forts at Hudson Bay. This attack made the English angry and they retaliated by sending a fleet of ships to attack Québec. When D'Iberville learned of the attack on Québec, he went by sea to sink the English ships in Hudson Bay.

From then on there was a lot of fighting between the English and French.

The Acadians: Sometimes the King of England and the King of France were fighting each other and sometimes they made peace for a time. The peace of 1713 gave the part of New France called Acadia to the English, but the Acadian settlers were mostly French. When the Acadians would not promise to be loyal to the English King, the new Governor of Acadia said, 'I'm sorry, you have to go and live somewhere else because there will soon be war again and you are dangerous to us.' The poor Acadians had to leave their homes.

War is very sad!

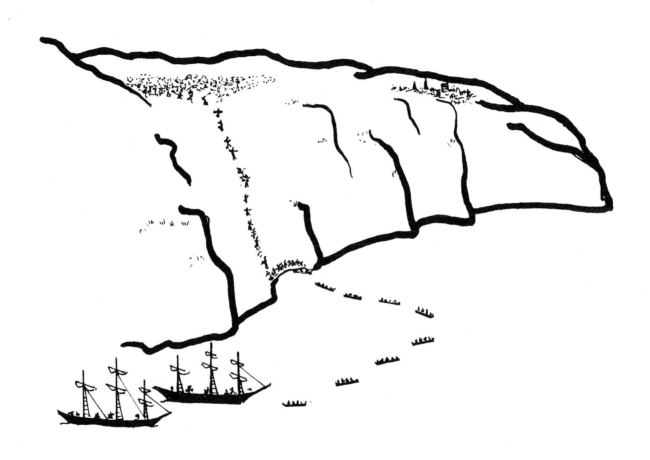

The Seven Years' War: And soon there was war again. This war is called the Seven Years' War. The French won some battles and the English won others. The English had more ships and in the summer of 1759 the English ships, with an army on board, sailed up the St. Lawrence to attack Québec. Québec was built on a steep cliff—impossible to climb and easy to defend.

For three months General Wolfe sailed his army up and down the river looking for a way to attack Québec. At last he found a little steep path and in the night the English soldiers climbed up the path to the top of the cliff. In the morning the surprised French found the English army outside their city. The French General, Montcalm, hurried his army into battle, but it was defeated and both brave generals were killed in the battle.

The war was over and the English had won. For a few years almost all of North America belonged to Britain, then thirteen colonies to the south revolted. They didn't want to belong to Britain any longer so they fought and won their War of Independence and became the United States of America. But the newly independent colonies were not satisfied. 'Why should Québec belong to England?' they said, 'we'll make it our Fourteenth Colony.' They sent two armies—one to besiege Québec and the other to invade Montréal. The Canadians didn't like their cities being invaded and besieged. 'Besides,' they said, 'we have a good peace treaty with the English King. We've kept our own language and laws and church.'

In the end, these Americans had to go back home and Canada remained a British colony.

The Loyalists Came to Canada: A great many people in the new United States had not wanted to revolt against the English King. They were called Loyalists because they had stayed loyal to Britain. Life was made miserable for them. They were attacked and driven from their homes and sometimes put into prison. 'Let's leave the new United States,' they said, 'and go and live under the British flag.' Thousands of the Loyalists went by ship from New York to Nova Scotia and hundreds of them travelled overland by cart to Québec with what they had been able to save from the fighting. The King gave the Loyalists land and money and supplies, but life was very hard. They had to start all over again; clearing trees, building cabins, and planting crops.

Now, for the first time, there were thousands of English speaking Canadians as well as French living in Québec, and they were not happy. 'We don't understand their language,' the English said, 'we don't go to the same church.' So the British Government divided the colony into two parts: Upper Canada—English speaking, which we call Ontario, and Lower Canada—French speaking, which we call Québec. The first Governor of Upper Canada was Colonel John Simcoe. He offered free land to anyone who wanted to come and settle. Many people accepted this offer and came to settle in Ontario.

Then the British Government divided Nova Scotia in two, because so many Loyalists had come, and it became Nova Scotia and New Brunswick. So, with Prince Edward Island and Newfoundland, there were now six British colonies.

Alexander Mackenzie Crosses Canada: Now that there was no more war, the struggle for the fur trade began again. A new company, called the North West Company, took over the old French routes and sent canoes farther and farther west to get the furs. One of the North West men, Alexander MacKenzie, travelled all the way to the Rocky Mountains by lake, river and portage. Then he crossed the mountains and came down to the Pacific, which is the ocean on that side of the country. Being the first white man to cross the continent made him very happy. He painted a sign on a rock by the beach that said: 'Alexander MacKenzie, from Canada by land, July 22, 1793.'

Captain Vancouver: Just before Alexander MacKenzie arrived at the Pacific by land, Captain George Vancouver got there by sea.

He was on his way up the Pacific coast of North America with orders from the British Government to make careful maps and charts of the west coast of Canada.

He was also told to take one last look for the Northwest Passage to China, which people had been looking for since the days of Cabot and Cartier. Vancouver went all the way up North to where the ice began, but there was no passage.

What a pity that Captain Vancouver and Alexander MacKenzie could not have met and talked. In those days, before the telephone and radio, there was no way they could have gotten in touch.

The Okanagan Pack-Train: Some years later two more fur trader-explorers, David Thompson and Simon Fraser, made their way towards the West Coast, building trading posts in the interior.

They were now very far from their bases on the Bay or in Montréal but much closer to the Pacific. Between these interior forts and the ocean were the huge Rocky Mountains.

In 1808 Simon Fraser managed to get down the terrible river which now bears his name. It was obvious that the Fraser, roaring down between canyon walls and full of rapids and whirlpools, could not be used as a route for freight canoes.

Farther south the lower part of the Columbia River flowed gently to the ocean. But there was no way to get there by canoe either.

So a trail was blazed between Fort Alexandria on the Fraser to Fort Okanagan on the Columbia. When the big canoes loaded with furs from the interior reached Alexandria, the voyageur paddlers turned themselves into pack riders and loaded their furs onto the backs of horses. Then they set off for Fort Kamloops where the company had a ranch. There they could rest and change horses before starting out again. The bells on the horses' harnesses jingled gaily and the voyageurs sang their old songs as they made their way across country to Fort Okanagan on the Columbia. Once there the packs were unloaded and put onto boats to be taken down to the Pacific Ocean.

The Okanagan Trail was 600 miles long. It was this last link, connecting with hundreds of miles of canoe trails, which gave Canada its first ocean-to-ocean highway.

The Selkirk Settlers: Meanwhile, far away in the East, settlers from Britain began to arrive to join the Loyalists from over the border. Lord Selkirk brought a group of Scots to farm in Prince Edward Island. It was good land and they did well, but the island was not big enough for everyone who wanted to come to Canada. So he bought a big piece of land from the Hudson's Bay Company and brought in more Scots.

This land was along the Red River at the edge of the great plains. It was rich land and the settlers were very happy with it. There were no trees to cut down; they just ploughed, sowed the seed and the crops grew. But there were other people who did not want farms on the plains.

The fur traders in Montréal were angry because dried buffalo meat provided the food for their long canoe trips. What would happen to the buffalo if the plains were turned into farms? And the Plains Indians and the Métis, who were half Indian and half white, made their living by hunting the buffalo. So they were angry too.

'How are we going to live,' they said, 'when the buffalo are gone?'

The Scottish homesteaders had a hard time. They were attacked and their farms were burned. In the end there was peace, and that was the beginning of Manitoba.

The War of 1812: Suddenly, however, there was war again between Canada and the United States. The Americans were angry with Britain and Britain was busy fighting against France. 'Now is our chance,' said the Americans, 'this time we'll get Canada.' They thought it would be easy to take Upper Canada because there were so many American settlers there. But their commander was not as clever as Canada's General Brock. And the Loyalists fought hard to stay Canadian. The Shawnee Indians, led by Tecumseh, came to help General Brock. Both Tecumseh and General Brock were killed, but their troops won the land battles in Upper Canada. General de Salaberry and the French Canadians won in Lower Canada and saved Montréal. The Americans sank British ships on the Lakes and burned Toronto; the British sank American ships at sea and burned the American capital of Washington. A lot of people hadn't wanted to fight this war at all!

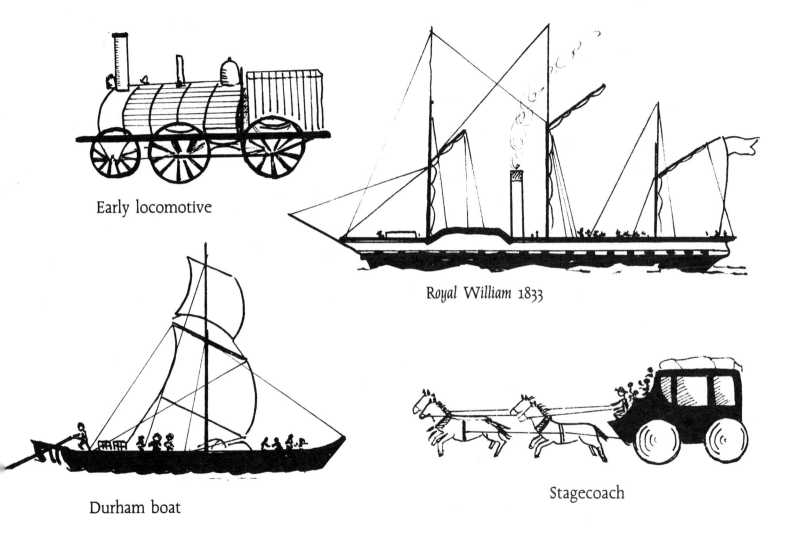

Early locomotive

Royal William 1833

Durham boat

Stagecoach

Transportation: After the war was over, more and more people came to Canada and soon there were roads between the towns, with wagons and stagecoaches travelling on them. And later on there were trains, which at first only ran in summer because the locomotives were not strong enough to get through the deep snow covering the tracks in winter. Flat-bottomed boats with sails took people and freight more comfortably up and down the rivers. Canals were built to let boats go around the rapids. And then there were steamers that at first had sails as well as engines, just to be safe in case of engine trouble. The first steamboat to cross the Atlantic was built in Canada. It was called the 'Royal William.' Once there were roads and railways and steamers, life was much more comfortable.

Gold in British Columbia: On the other side of the Rockies the little trading posts on the mainland and on Vancouver Island were growing very slowly because they were so very, very far away from settlements in the East. People and supplies coming by ship had to go all the way around the bottom of South America and then up the west coast of South America and North America until they got to the west coast of Canada. Very few people came.

Suddenly, in 1858, gold was discovered on the mainland and there was a great rush of gold seekers, mostly American miners from the California gold fields. Because there were only a few Hudson's Bay people to keep law and order, the British government quickly made British Columbia into a colony, sent a governor and ordered roads and bridges to be built.

Many prospectors didn't find any gold, but they stayed to farm and fish in the mild climate of the beautiful colony.

Newfoundland: Not much has been said about Newfoundland. Do you remember the big island on the Atlantic Ocean side of Canada, where the Vikings stayed for three years?

Five hundred years after the Vikings had come and gone, Cabot had come looking for a way to China. He wrote letters about the millions of fish in the sea near Newfoundland and fishermen began coming every spring from England, France, Spain and Portugal.

No one country owned the island. The captain of whichever ship arrived first was called the 'Admiral' and he was the boss for that summer. Some fishermen went ashore to dry their fish and soon there were a few settlements. The biggest settlements were St. John's and Placentia.

In 1583 Sir Humphrey Gilbert went ashore at St. John's and claimed it for Queen Elizabeth of England. France took another part of the island. The fishing companies did not want year-round settlers on the land. They wanted to keep all the fish for themselves when they came in the summertime. They persuaded the government to pass laws to stop people from settling there.

In 1637 Charles I gave Newfoundland to a group headed by Sir David Kirke, who became the first Governor. But the French and English still raided each other's fishing ports and settlements.

At last, when all the fighting was over, people were allowed to settle and farm, and they got rid of the Admirals' rule. People wanted their own government. It took a long time but at last they succeeded in becoming a colony with its own Governor, Council and Assembly.

Confederation: Now there were seven colonies—New Brunswick, Lower Canada, Upper Canada, British Columbia, Newfoundland, Nova Scotia and Prince Edward Island—all busy growing, farming and trading separately. The people in the older colonies were beginning to think it might be a good idea to join in order to be stronger. The people of Nova Scotia, Prince Edward Island and New Brunswick were the first ones to talk about it. Then John A. Macdonald from Upper Canada had his great idea. 'Let's *all* join,' he said, 'so that we can protect ourselves better.' He was so sure that his idea was right that he persuaded the leaders of the other provinces to agree with his idea. Naturally, there was a lot of arguing and quarrelling. Prince Edward Island and Newfoundland wouldn't join. But the other colonies agreed and for the first time there was a Nation of Canada with a central government at Ottawa.

Cross Canada Railway: At first there was no thought of British Columbia's joining because it was so far away and there was all that space of empty prairies between them and the rest of the country.

Some people in British Columbia wanted to join the United States.

'We're much closer to the States,' they said; 'we don't even have a proper road joining us to the rest of the country.'

But John A. Macdonald had the answer to that.

'If you will join us,' he said, 'we will build a railroad right across the country to bring us all together.'

They agreed and joined the Confederation. Two years later Prince Edward Island joined too.

The Prairies: So there was Canada in 1870 — one nation from coast to coast. In the East, as far west as Winnipeg there were British, French, Americans and native Indians; in the West there were British, Americans and Indians.

And between the Red River and the Rockies lay the great lone land, the prairies — empty but for Indians and Métis and the roaming buffalo. It was Hudson's Bay land and the company didn't want farms on the prairies. In Europe hundreds of people wanted to farm but they had no land. They wanted to come to Canada.

The Canadian Government bought the land from the Hudson's Bay Company and encouraged people to come. And they came — by ship, then by train as far as the railway could take them, and then in the squeaky, two-wheeled Red River carts which could travel on the roadless prairies.

There were so few trees on the prairies that many people made their first homes out of sod; some even dug underground homes and roofed them over. The newcomers were hard workers and the land was so good they soon had good farms and good crops.

Rebellion and the Mounties: Of course, there were troubles. When the Government sent people to measure and divide up the Red River country, the Métis were upset. They wanted rights to the land they were living on but no one in Ottawa took any notice of their request. When a governor arrived, they rose in rebellion and would not let him in. They started a government of their own with Louis Riel, a Métis, as President.

Ottawa then dispatched soldiers to put an end to Riel's government, which had lasted for eight months. He fled to the United States and the Ottawa Government made the Red River country into the Province of Manitoba and gave each of the Métis two hundred and forty acres of land. Those who preferred a wilderness life where there was no government moved farther west.

Because there was no one to keep order on the prairies, the Government ruled that a mounted police force would be sent to take charge. It left Manitoba on horseback in June 1874 and rode a thousand miles across the prairies. The policemen looked splendid in their scarlet, gold and grey uniforms.

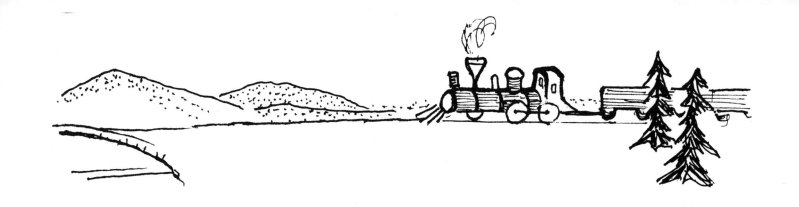

The Second Métis Rebellion and the Railroad: All this time the Government had been struggling to have the railroad built. It was a terrible job—over rocky plateaus and swamps and through forests, mountains and gorges. It cost millions of dollars and the people of British Columbia were getting impatient. 'Where is the railroad we were promised?' they asked.

It was coming as fast as it could but there was never enough money. Even so it was coming too fast for the Métis of the West. They did not want it. It was the same problem all over again: they were afraid they would lose their land. They rebelled again and in 1885 sent for Louis Riel to come back as their leader. They also sent messages to other Indian tribes, urging them to rise up and drive the white man out.

Now everyone could see how important the railroad was. It took soldiers four days to get from Kingston to Winnipeg instead of the endless weeks it normally would have taken. Farther west, where there were gaps in the line, rails were laid on snow or ice. Seven weeks after it had started, the rebellion was over.

The railroad was finished and, though Canada had only four and half million people, it had the longest railroad in the world. With trains running from coast to coast and with so many people coming to settle on the prairies, the Government created two new provinces: Alberta and Saskatchewan.

The Yukon and the Northwest Territories: If you look at the map you can see that almost all of Canada had now been divided into provinces—all except for the huge treeless and cold area north of the mountains, lakes and prairies.

When gold was found near the Klondike River in the Yukon, it brought another rush of miners and traders. The Government then set up the Yukon Territory so that there would be proper law and order.

The rest was left as the Northwest Territories: mostly lakes, swamps, and tundra. Not many people lived there, but it was home to Eskimos, trappers and hunters of the caribou.

We have inherited one of the most beautiful countries in the world—mountains, rivers, forests, lakes and plains, now strung together by roads, railways and aircraft.

When we think of the vision, courage and hard work of all these brave people we have been reading about, we have to ask ourselves, 'What can we do, each one of us, to keep our Canada beautiful and strong?'

KARIN MOORHOUSE was in 1905 born of Swedish parents in England and educated there and in Switzerland.

She worked for a few years in Paris and for a short time in Poland. Then she married and came to Canada with her husband in 1932. They lived for the first five years in Toronto, where they became involved with Andrew Allan's early radio drama. Then they moved to Montréal. She was a founding member of a still-flourishing theatre group and of a literary group responsible for the creation of the Pointe Claire public library.

During these years they had three children. Her husband in the last ten years of his life became a professional producer and director of documentary films, in which work she was able to help him. At his early death, she went back to teaching.

Later, she wrote and narrated a short history series for children for CBC television called 'Once upon a Country.' Though she has written articles, this is her first book. Karin Moorhouse passed away in 1994.